Against information

and other poems

John Lane

New Native Press

1995

Copyright © John Lane 1995

All Rights Reserved

FIRST PRINTING

Some of these poems have appeared in *Point* ("Against Information"), *Nexus* ("Light" which is titled "Darkness" in this text), *The Wofford Journal* ("Childhood & Linguistics"), *House Organ* ("The Muse Is Looking For").

A limited edition broadside of "Against Information" was published by New Native Press in May, 1994.

Portions of "Against Information" were first broadcast on National Public Radio and the Canadian Broadcasting System in September, 1994.

ACKNOWLEDGEMENTS

Thanks to Nan Watkins for proofreading and editorial ideas; to the Suite Of Peripheral Studies at Wofford College; to Cristina Del Sesto at Corporation for Public Broadcasting; WNCW for airtime given to "Against Information"; to Leonard Cohen for "The Future" and Van Morrison for "No Guru, No Teacher, No Method" which served as literal background inspiration for these poems; to Greg Olson who was the music behind the madness; and to Mark Olencki—the photographic eye behind the blind rush of words.

Cover and book design by Dana Irwin, Irwin Design; Asheville, North Carolina.

Back cover photo of John Lane by Mark Olencki.

New Native books and broadsides are published for Thomas Rain Crowe and New Native Press. All orders and correspondence should be addressed to: P.O. Box 661, Cullowhee, N.C. 28723 (704-293-9237) USA.

ISBN # 1-883197-06-6

Library of Congress Catalog Card #: 94-069299

Against Information
& Other Poems

OTHER BOOKS BY JOHN LANE

Thin Creek

Quarries

Body Poems

As The World Around Us Sleeps

Weed Time

CONTENTS

PREFACE 7

I.
AGAINST INFORMATION

Against Information	10
The Peripheral Poets: A Manifesto	17
Cellular Phones	18
Telephone Access Codes	20
Dayrunners	21
Reduced Fat	23
Health Care Plan	24
Rising And Falling Stock	26
The Bottom Line	28
Darkness	29
College Textbooks	31
The Old Professor	33
The Well-Rounded Student Speaks	35
Sooner Than We Think	36
Couplets	37
The Career Track	38
Sweet Tea	39
Death	41

II.
EVEN IN DOGGEREL THERE IS THIS SEED

The Early Decades	44
Hammered Leaves	46
Six Words Off A Postcard By Nin Andrews	48
The Map	50
Connemara	51
Nostalgia For Work And Deep Mountains	53
Good Fences	55
Childhood & Linguistics	56
My Dead Father Surveys The Patterns	57
Someday My Mother's Death	58
The Muse Is Looking For	59
Rhetoric	60
Doggerel	61
Theory In A Public Place	62
Logging	63
Sailboat	64

ABOUT THE AUTHOR   67

PREFACE

John Lane is a young Carolina poet at Wofford. Early in '94 Thomas Crowe's New Native Press up in Cullowhee, NC printed Lane's longish poem, "Against Information."

It's a fine poem, a controlled histrionic tinged with anti-technology sentiments that would have done the Luddite and Agrarian movements proud. Lane wafts it with Whitmanesque exuberances. It takes issue with the loss of poetry, desire, and spontaneity in our lives, as they are replaced by consuming interests in consumption and career paths.

"I have rewritten the Bill of Dreams in the left ventricle/of the human heart," Lane tells us. *"I have etched a new compact there/with a laser finer than sunlight."*

The poem covers eight pages in its $1.00 fold-out edition. When Lane read it at The Green Door in Asheville, over a hundred people paid $5 each to hear him.

Down in Columbia, SC Lane's poem caught the eye of Brett Bursey, editor of *Point*, a moderately-left 20-page tabloid popular among the avant-garde, who got permission to reprint the poem on a two-page spread in the June 1994 edition. It appeared in an attractive format, with a few little illustrations.

It is not traditional rhymed poetry. In fact, except for each stanza beginning with its first line set back, one could easily think the stanzas are prose paragraphs.

Which, in fact, is exactly what appears to have happened once the poem reached *Point*'s several thousand readers.

The poem starts off with a headline like a news announcement:

"New Satellite Dishes"

Then this message follows:

> *Today the next satellite dish is announced,*
> *"pizza-sized," 18 inches across, pulls in*
> *150 channels, mounts on rooftop, railing,*
> *windowsill, $699.95, includes decoder box*
> *and remote control.*

Then, regular type is used for the next stanza, which seems to explain what in the preceding one could have been taken as an advertisement:

> This is the latest machinery. This is the council
> of technicians. User friendly. Installs inminutes.
> No adjustments necessary. Lifetime

> guarantee. Call now for a free demonstration.
> 1-800-555-DISH. The greatest innovation since
> the tractor. Get rid of the old dish in your
> yard. Plant seedlings in it. You out there
> in Iowa, feed your hogs from the bowl. In
> California, fill it with water for a pool.
> Or put it in your barn, in the attic like
> your grandmother's hatbox.

It is important to this story that we understand that Lane's television satellite dish at that time was entirely in his head, an imaginary product dreamed up to portray the enemy against which the bulk of the poem inveighs.

Unfortunately, the readers of *Point* missed this point.

The first clue that the poem was being misread came from a little old lady who called the editor to complain about false advertising. She had, she said, wanted to get the new miracle television receiver and to convert her larger and older one into a food or water dish for her dog. But when she called the 800 number in the "ad" (Lane's poem), she had been told they had no such product for sale.

Curious that Lane may have accidentally used an actual 800 number in his poem, the editor called the number himself.

Lo and behold, it was a live number.

Not only that. It belongs to a bait company in Kentucky, the owner of which was very exercised about the cause of the 200 inquiry calls he had received wanting to order $699.95 pizza-sized satellite dishes.

The most encouraging thing in this whole episode is the hard evidence that people still read poetry. Most marketing experts would agree that getting 200 callers from a reference in a relatively obscure monthly tabloid would indicate that at least 10,000 people had read it.

With that big an audience, maybe Lane's alarm about the death of poetry in this careerist technocratic age is premature.

We'll settle for believing thousands of people did read it. It's irrelevant that they don't seem to have understood it.

Poetry lives.

That's an important victory for the John Lane Quixotes of the world. Never mind if the poetry readers seem to want to buy satellite dishes. Let's just bask in that possibility of poetry having a big audience.

—Larry McGehee
syndicated column "Southern Seen"
July 17, 1994

I. AGAINST INFORMATION

"The Age demanded..."
—EZRA POUND

AGAINST INFORMATION

I. NEW SATELLITE DISHES

*Today the next satellite dish is announced,
"pizza-sized," 18 inches across, pulls in
150 channels, mounts on rooftop, railing,
windowsill, $699.95, includes decoder box
and remote control.*

This is the latest machinery. This is the council of technicians.
>User friendly. Installs in minutes. No adjustments necessary.
Lifetime guarantee. Call now for a free demonstration.
1-800-555-DISH. The greatest innovation since the tractor.
Get rid of the old dish in your yard. Plant seedlings
in it. You out there in Iowa, feed your hogs from the bowl.
In California, fill it with water for a pool, or put it
in the barn, in the attic like your grandmother's hatbox.

The old dish is the Olduvai Gorge of past entertainment,
>the last empire charged on your credit card, the Hindenburg
of information, the Pony Express of movies, the siege
catapult of sports. This is the Age of Information
and smaller machinery clears all misunderstandings about
who won the Series, the latest theories on evolution,
the number of American medals at the Olympics, the sexual
orientation of Michael Jackson, and who is president.
Right now someone is mounting the new pizza dish,
somewhere else there is an English muffin dish, a silver
dollar dish, a dish the size of a dime. And next
to the easy chair rests a new decoder with 500 channels.

And from the glowing screen somewhere a man speaks in a hundred
>voices about the coming of Christ, another of the Serengeti,
another of measles and the Home Pharmacy. Don't open
your hearts to "Car Talk." Fall on your knees for diversity.
Don't punch from AM to FM. The pale hand taps a remote,
the circuits respond like Lippizaner stallions. In Sarajevo
the radio broadcasts men walking through snow. The signal
bounces off cloud cover, huddles like rats in the condensers.

On cable a former beauty queen adjusts her makeup, air time
>moments away, the satellites poised above, the recoilless

rifles asleep in caves in the hillside. The howitzers
trundling over ruts to the rear. The beauty queen's
waist is thin as a mortar shell. Her technician counts
to ten backwards as the satellite pivots in space.

Welcome to the war. Welcome to the future. Welcome
all of you out there in Iowa who have just tuned in.
I lift a signal from one of the former garden spots.
I stand here lighter than the year I won the title.
I laugh when it is appropriate. I bleed when called.
My blond hair is styled in the midst of war and rape.
My fingernails are not broken. I'd eat three squares
if not dieting. I'd fly to Paris to diddle my boyfriend.
I'd drink water hauled in by jet from some other world.

II. RESUMÉS FOR POETS

Yesterday in the mail a friend sends ten resumés
of poets, dense, endless lists of publications,
jobs and education.

The slow drift of lives across paper, the black ink
of ambition, the alphabetical staircase of greed,
the pedigree of corruption, hand-to-hand, the buddy,
the crony, the slap-my-back-I'll-slap-yours
network we need for hiring. The pages
more real than a body. The trespass of image
and the urban sympathy of committees. The trees
cut down and processed. The trucks. The diesel fuel.
The chain saws. The dry rot. The loam. The earthworms
uprooted and listed under education. The pine
warblers cited like foundation grants. The Guggenheim
of endless streams running muddy with silt. The **NEA**'s
fire break channeling obscenity past careers and money.
The white space, speaking of institutional loneliness,
and dark type screaming of the rage of tenured fathers.

Fed Ex all resumés back to their organic source!
> Reconstitute the forests. Cancel all poetry classes
> and workshops! Two Douglas fir for the Iowa workshop!
> A loblolly and slash pine for the Johns Hopkins seminars!
> Eight western cedar and a Manzanita for the low residency
> MFAs! I am the new prophet of a pulpless ambition!
> I am the last photocopier to blindly collate
> multiple submissions! I am the last poem published
> in *The New Yorker* and listed for hire! My resumé empties
> itself monthly! Each week I exhaust the need
> for another entry under publications! I drain
> the sap back to the trunk! I worry the toner
> into multiple components unusable by me!
> I do not staple, fold, or crimp the corner!
> I do not stand in line for return postage!

III. MORE MEMORY

"Apple announces the Super Mac with super memory..."
                —AP NEWS ITEM

I announce the digital machine's memory is a meddling list.
> The file server hums as it runs on the electric current
> of time. The file server spins on days and days, indexing
> the past, present, and future. Everything fits, everything
> in alphabetical order, scanned for virus, displayed
> in 640 colors on the screen. I announce the first computer
> invective that doesn't scan for virus. I announce lessening
> all memory. I announce forgetting. This poem is breathing,
> without virtual memory, without Windows. When this poem
> becomes a computer it will run no DOS, with RAM headed
> in the wrong direction, with dual floppies, no hard drive,
> a dot matrix printer, with software still at the 1.0 level.

This is the ancient software update of *what if*:
> *What if* the silicon drained back to the white beach?

What if the waves washed grooves in all microchips?
What if computers could be lodged in the hinge of an oyster?
What if the apple rotted and the worms of pencils crawled
through the flesh? Then I would type my name with
the syllables of breath. Then I would feel dirt under
my finger tips, my prints new as a software update.
Then I would reinhabit Plato's cave, and Heidegger's
schoolhouse. Then I would stand with Wordsworth in the glen.
This day I announce the software of syllabics, dactyls,
spondees and iambics like keys on a keyboard. I announce
the hard drive of tradition, the ROM of books, the program
of handwriting, a code to be broken anew, memory of book-
stores, the motherboard of a comfortable chair, silence
and time. The virtual reality of a walk in the woods.
The workshop of hands on a chest. The laptop of scattered
love. The modem of desire. The e-mail of old letters.

IV. ORDER

*"Simple events give rise to complex systems
and complex events give rise to simple results."*
—A PHYSICS *CD*-ROM

Rising in the distance is a complex mountain range.
    Rising nearby is a garden in springtime.
    Rising from my desk is a simple mote of dust.
    Rising tomorrow is a sun I'd call possibility.
    Rising water is a sign of heavy rain.

Rain is the seasonal sign of patterns we call weather.
    Weather is infinite sadness when connected to love.
    Blue days are memories of solitude.
    Solitude is the last refuge of endangered grief.
    Rising always behind us is the memory of childhood.

Forgetting is like a child's wagon or the programming
    on a channel with bad reception. A reception

    is not always the place to offer invective like this.
    I am like a computer indexing a long manuscript,
    running all night in the professor's office,
    the words falling into place like rain in a puddle.
    And what of the order of sadness, the order of unknowing?
    The mind follows the thought through one course until
    it rests like the anthropologist tracking the ape
    through a day in the treetops. She looks at her journal,
    traces each impulse back to the source, order today,
    order tomorrow, order when the sun rises and sets.

Order today for a special offer. Order today and get the power
    of complexity and chaos. Order today for the knives of blood
    and intuition. Order today for the multimedia of Picasso,
    Blake, and Jung. Order today for the printing press.
    Order today and I'll ship Second Day Air. Turn quickly to
    the page of your absolute longing. Get out your beads
    for trade. Order today.

V. CERTAINTY

"Sooner murder an infant in its cradle than
nurse unacted desires."
        —WILLIAM BLAKE

I have rewritten the Bill of Dreams in the left ventricle
    of the human heart. I have etched a new compact there
    with a laser finer than sunlight. I have spelled
    all the words with exploding vowels to enrich the blood
    for travel and uncertainty. I have set the heart in motion
    again after this major surgery. I have floated
    the last college student's unacted desire to the level
    of dogma. I have posted all jobs on speculation, even
    the jobs reserved for the soul-hungry. I reconstitute
    the Underclass of Waking Dreams. I assemble the young
    lonely lost men without MasterCards or Money Market
    reserved in their names upon graduation. I rent

and never own. I drive an old truck, paid for in the '50s
by an Indian in Nevada with no belt and a bad hangover.

There was never a logic of career. There was only the seed,
always subject to weather. There were always graphs,
job listings, quotas, and the market. But there was
always behind the abstractions a field called chance,
a range of hills where you could lose the present.
This we call *finding your way* in our language.
This we call *the wandering among opposites, the old
clanging rocks, the journey, the search, the pilgrimage,
the walk-about,* and this we endorse over the perfect resumé,
a suit and tie, a second interview, a free business lunch.

I reject all economic metaphors but return. I reject bottom
line, profit, short and long run, interest, but not return;
I reject dividend, currency, liquid assets, bankruptcy,
GNP, the stock market, standard of living, the check-out
counter, but not return; I reject change, progress, money,
production, packaging, buying and selling, worth,
economics, territory, democracy, education. I maintain
return, and in the place of all other choices I slip
the pulse of the heart, the implicating wind, mystery
of origin, the timid choice that leads to bounty,
the bountiful rejection in the face of ages of logic,
soft collars, soft sell, wet nest, the timid voice,
resumés not postmarked in time for the grand prize,
timeless needs like desire.

Now I return to certainty: the paths beaten dusty by years
of fearful travel, blackberries picked nearest the road,
the easy ten pounds lost to the latest diet, books long
on the best seller list about what men fear, reading
assignments with no teeth, tests in fraternity files,
Friday night parties and the hangovers that follow.
I return like Blake to desire. I return to the impulse
of personal knowing. I return to the escape from parents
and elders. I return to Oedipus and his mother.
I postpone the complex, and embrace the dark.
I don't write away for more information. I take

a job in a restaurant and own one suit of clothes.
I wait on tables and make love late in the morning.
I don't see my life closing in at thirty. I don't
respond to requests for money from my alma mater.
I return my parent's calls, but melt down the extra
key. I own an impractical dog, a greyhound
in trauma from racing. I know people on drugs in spite
of the war. My opinions are revolting to textile
interns. My draft card has been washed. I believe
in a cash economy and worship folding money.
I quote China as a model for simplicity.

And for desire? The blood in any muscle. What dries first
in a child. What is easily lost sight of in the storm
of allegiances like college and family. Future pulsing
the present if you listen for the slurring sound
in the chest. It is mistakes and surprises.
Not the implicated step or the path with handrail.
Always turns in a padded swivel. It is what hinges before
the rust sets out to close the mechanical gap.
Desire is the hydraulics of deep need. Desire is the only
channel open of silt, the only canal open to the one alone.
It is Blake's original and only essential crime,
and it is mine.

THE PERIPHERAL POETS: A MANIFESTO

We do not need to sit on the desk top. We remain connected
    only by cables to the main frame, but we will not
    give up our clutch of cables. If we are in programs,
    they are ones with small budgets which run like the
    Volkswagen of old with burnt valves and one firing
    cylinder. Our publicity is printed at the local shop.
    Our books just as soon letter pressed as squeezed
    from a newer machine. We have unhealthy allegiances
    to bookstores. We understand Snyder's references
    to bio-region, and clean our tools for more work.

We are not the motherboard, which we know instructs our
    passion's delicate tracking of some invisible groove.
    We are the laser reading, not the corrupt surface
    where the clutter of tradition skips the light
    from scene-to-scene. We do not deny tradition,
    but lean against it, the way Thoreau walked
    the paths around Concord woods after burning them down.
    Where is the fatherboard in the new science?
    Where are the boards for children and priests?
    These are questions peripheral to the age
    but we will ask them with no promise of answers.

We do not value answers as much as questions. This is the Age
    of Questions spreading like cane in the creek bottoms.
    This is the age of Rilke and the lost words returning.
    We make no rules, but one: plug in, but not always.
    Have your machine running in a back room. Be a file
    server, but keep only the regular hours of your body's
    deepest need. Regular hours are the blood of commerce.

CELLULAR PHONES

*after talking with a friend on a cellular phone,
and realizing it was my first time*

At the edge of the service zone the signal gets weakest.
    At the edge of a culture a woman places a black
    receiver back in the cradle. A man listens for birds
    in the yard. The signal will return. The woman will
    speak again. It is the middle of the latest shift.
    The highway will remain smooth for miles. The median
    trimmed by a farmer, hay for his cattle, hay for sale.

At the edge of the signal there is no elevated conversation,
    no one works at an alternative to obsolete notions,
    the only context is the music of the car's motion,
    noise at the margin of fields along the interstate.
    Call the rabbits within your cell! Call all dead raccoons
    along the long highway! Dial up the bobcat hunkering
    in shadows when the locked car passes at sixty-five!

A cellular zone is a long wireless dreamscape. Cellular
    voices speak from the tunnel of reception where
    the dream of safety for mothers is perpetrated around
    utility fires, and traveling children like Boy Scouts
    trust electricity's merit. A web we touch, never in
    the mobile middle. A spider indifferent to weather.
    Oceans' tides not monitored. Certainty's storm surge.

Yes, I doubt the king's latest kingdom. I offer suspicion
    like bad reception toward the machinery of industry.
    I heap doubt on all new inventions that propose to only
    connect. I levy uncertainty on being in touch. I am
    skeptical of progress. Show me the fossil record. I want
    soft tissue proof, not bones disturbed by checking
    accounts, marketing plans, phone cells, exclusive rate
    plans, free leatherette cases, specials at Radio Shack.

I am the archeologist of older incantations. I look
        to the caves by desert lakes. There I will find
        communication rolled on papyrus and stored vertically
        in crumbling clay jars. The Third Kingdom has passed.
        I listen as the wagons of literacy pause on the road.
        They are headed to the front, and the last poet is
        asleep in the loose hay. The stars are all satellites.
        Near Sarajevo the generals talk on cellular phones.
        Near Atlanta the salespeople stand poised for the trade
        wars. Their cellular attachments are free of wires.
        Their wireless wives and husbands at the entrance
        to a shortening code. They hand off fading service.
        They can call from anywhere, even a thunderstorm,
        the bowels of the ox of last month's latest circuits.

Enter the special access code now. Enter a notion T. S. Eliot
        would know. And Tu Fu. And the woman pounding papyrus.
        Go on with your calls. I am not dialing for cessation,
        not turning back, not abandoning the impulse toward
        change, not claiming prior right for the symbolic
        kingdom of ink and vegetable pulp, not sharpening
        a box full of turkey quills. But I question genocide,
        even the genocide of old technology and greetings.
        I am suspicious of education comfortable with industry,
        of men and women always in touch. Here I punch
        in my code. Here I get in touch once, here I register
        a last call from the road, here, an inner logic left
        at the sound of the beep. Here is my listed number.

TELEPHONE ACCESS CODES

"Don't leave home without it."
—AD FOR AMERICAN EXPRESS CARD

The protocol is a first leaf glued to the manuscript, the first
    kiss, the series of numbers, the established ceremonial forms,
    the courtesies, shaman's drum, guitar strings running top
    to bottom. The tie, resumé, paying for gas first, asking
    for permission to proceed. Asking for need. Worrying
    the forms, not the content. If the shoe fits, bear it.
    If the shoe fits, it was cut from a mold. Among the ministers
    of electronic culture a digit pressed into the dial can deny
    entry. Among the grand deans strings of digits cavort
    for entry to the system. Admit one. Or admit none.

We with protocol have made our call. The circuits respond.
    The signal moves like thought across the cables.
    My home is wired to receive all incoming calls
    with the right protocol. I am in touch with the wrinkled
    belly of access and protocol is the place to apply
    the scratch. We place the protractor on the angle
    and measure for distance. We are ninety degrees
    from the center of the service. We can hear
    the electronic drum perfectly well from our seat.
    I record the voice with a hand recorder and check the profile.
    I punch in the special access code. I'm alive. The drum
    is alive. It is amplified. The Greek way was to stand
    at the stage's middle. My way is the rotary dial.

DAYRUNNERS

The Time Management System/The Project Organizer
Objectives/Contacts/Finances/Monthly calendar
4-year overview/charting capacity

What would happen if all the Dayrunners exploded?
    What would be lost if pages did not have lines?
    How would we organize without a calendar?
    What would be lost? Production would decline.
    But what really depends on production? I'm speaking
    of the grass. I'm speaking of the rabbit not in a cage.
    I'm not speaking of a new BMW plant with trucks
    that ballet back and forth with concrete for the
    opening. I'm not speaking of training camps for
    football, or a new way to advertise gold. I stopped
    speaking of those things when I closed my Dayrunner.

We lie when we speak of organization. It is the great lie
    if we believe it is possible. Half of the day is chaos
    and will remain so. There is no time to be saved. Jesus
    tried that. His plan was eternity. He indexed an age.
    And we set out to make appointments on time. On time?
    We know nothing. We are all late. Even Jesus arrived
    at the tomb late. Moses broke the tablets. Noah pulled
    up the plank and set sail. He didn't know when the rain
    would stop or what he would do to feed all those
    animals. He did not check his black Dayrunner for
    appointments. He watched 40 days for the clearing.

A day is a holy thing. A day is the fold time makes
    in the cloth of our lives. A day is the comfortable
    shirt we put on unironed. Love the days. Let days
    gather slowly like spring pollen among us. Let them rot
    like fall leaves in the compost. Give days distinction,
    but not the distinction of schedules. Close the black
    Dayrunners forever and score the sections shut with
    the strongest velcro. Give up on the accountancy of

"the Classic edition." Do not plan. Do not check your
calendar or make notes on the Memo-ry pages. A day
has no memory. A day has nothing but the moment.

You will open up to the dawn. You will see the sun after
floating. You will not worry the landscape of your
father's cheek. Your mother will not schedule you
for the Junior League. You will not live in a shapeless
house in the outer suburbs. You will not drive the same
car as your accountant neighbor or wear a blue suit
or travel on an expense account. You will run but it
will not be for a day. You will run for eternity.
You will organize nothing manageable. There will be
no business cards in the provided vinyl pockets.

All my pages are unlined. I sit in the ark and wait
for the rain to stop. I will write my schedule in
the new mud. I will follow the crane inland. I will
start over again with an emphasis on too much space.
There will be no talk of planning. Towns will grow
out of our dreams. The village will have a circle,
not square. I will manage the sky's blue bowl.
I will make valuable contacts with the remaining
trees. The finances will be stable if my only
long-term gain will be erosion. The old charts will
surface finally from the flooded museums. They chart
the islands to our east. They chart anything but
human ambition or mutual funds. I will stop here
because it becomes very clear I am not organized.

REDUCED FAT

I am the Johnny Appleseed of fat, carrying the fat sack over
    my shoulder. In it are doughnuts from Harris Teeter,
    an eclair made of real cream, Half & Half, a steak,
    two chickens with the skin attached. These are not
    heroin or crack. This is the food your grandmother
    ate. This is the latest object of the purist's desire.
    This is the one thin god slaying all others, the church
    built over the temple in the grove.

Body fat is the new war against yourselves, and are you
    to be its foot soldier? Nothing has changed. There is no
    discovery in the lab. Fat has always been fat. To watch
    it and to banish it from the kingdom are different acts.
    Ask to see the King's pantry. Comb through the garnishes,
    write proclamations as to who can pinch an inch, anoint
    the gram and make it holy. Found a state religion
    on the thin and tan in January.

This is the way to bring fat to a halt. This is the way
    to send a message to the court of the body. Fat is a Christ.
    Excess is the cross. The guards will gamble for fat's clothes
    when he is nailed to the cross beams. After three days fat
    rises from the tomb and takes his place among the fallen
    thieves. Fat ascends, leaving the message of the saints
    on the earth below: holy! holy! holy! Holy, the lonely ones
    who do not count the grams. Holy, the waistline of the Buddha.
    Holy, the burning butter and bread. Holy, ice cream
    and its royal glow. Holy, candy bar when it is up we need
    to rise. Holy, chocolate milk. Holy! holy! holy! All is holy!
    Even the fat at my sides!

HEALTH CARE PLAN

"Safe in their Alabaster Chambers—
Untouched by morning—
And untouched by Noon—
Lie the meek members of the Resurrection—
                    —EMILY DICKINSON

Antibiotics are burning a hole in my sleep. I am sweeping
    the cave of illness. I dream the dog has used the other
    room to escape my training, and a snake slips into a
    rain puddle shadowed by a single creosote bush. As you
    can see I am not alone, even though the small pill has
    cleansed my system of biotics. I have killed a multitude
    whose destinies cross mine. I choose to clear them out.
    As biology, I am never alone, walking the edges
    of my fitness and health, carrying always this colony
    on the bus of my body. It is Mexico in there. It is not
    the freeways of a populous suburb. We can never clean
    the living cells of the multitude of afflictions. Some
    illness is ready to board the bus at any station.

Some disturbance wakes me, and the snake is swimming toward
    the bed, unstoppable by my hoe. I drink the glass of
    water from the table. Tomorrow, if the plan has worked,
    I'll stand cured for prolonged conversation. The snake
    enters the pool of my sleep. The bus leaves the station
    again. I invest the yield of fitful sleep. I dream:

There is a city growing on the tallest hill like Las Vegas.
    In it there is a Heart Center, Ambulatory Care,
    an Emergency Room, wards for the wounded, wards
    for the fathers with Alzheimer's who walk around
    nude in the hallways. There are nurses and doctors,
    and then at the very top, there are the merchants.
    Their offices are abstract and connected by hallways
    to the banks. They gamble among the commodities
    of the body: blood, tissue, the current pulsing
    between. They plan for their retirement. They feel
    secure in their positions, pushing their ambition
    for space and assets into the shadows of distant bodies.

More rooms for the old ones lost to cigarettes! A CAT scan
   for a senator delivered from divorce! The sun and moon
   are on dialysis and the state will not pick up the bill!
   Who has a kidney for hire to the last planet discovered
   this century? Whose plan offers dental care to the teeth
   of the Bill of Rights? Mapplethorpe's portraits are in
   the National Gallery, crippled by the Second Amendment.
   The President has a fever from Arkansas. His wife
   articulates the mystery of health and law by his bedside.

I propose these solutions: attention to the body. The slowing
   down of choice like a heartbeat. The imminent doorway
   of pure desire. Emergency service for the poor operating
   gladly at a loss. The delivery of love like a laser.
   Proper causeways over the lake of our indifference.
   Removing the merchants from our dreams, and educating
   first our doctors in the stories of Chekhov, not numbers.

RISING AND FALLING STOCK

*"Tao brings the principles of all things
into single agreement."*
—Han Fei Tzu

March madness continues and the brokers consult the blinking
    cursor like Mayan priests tracking the rising planet
    Venus. The market has dropped by 16%. The brightest
    star pulls free of the tree line over Cuba. In the halls
    of finance the men in shirt sleeves worry the landscape
    known for perfect mathematical gain. Among stone arches
    the priests calculate to the lonely zero. The ancient
    Dow of the long count has been running for millions of
    seasons, rising and falling with Venus. On Wall Street
    stock is traded from the basement of impulse, hands
    reaching from the towers. The holy books are full of
    charts and graphs. The averages speak of loss and gain.
    The peasants go on with their grinding. The priests
    sleep all day in the royal chambers, dreaming the night
    sky. The yearly tracks of Venus clutter their sleep,
    a clicking digital ceremony, a feathery calculated god.

Can I not speak of the old Tao, the Water Course Way, or is
    it too late in the age? I own no stock. I do not chart
    Venus, hold no chamber for the daily rest. I take routes
    preferred by water, slide under the stationary stone.
    And if the men in shirt sleeves trouble my course with
    the cobble of finance, I slide over their shallows
    with my own flood. I choose the simple Water Course Way.
    The markets are pulsing. I do not listen to affluence.
    I dig under the stump for the spring's opening.
    I draw my water from where the water breaks free
    of the darkness. I look to the grounding flow, not
    stars or the numbers spun like a thread from the
    spider's belly. I tilt the old tin cup that hangs
    on the forked hickory branch. I follow the water
    as it meets the divided flow, the multiple sparing

    of branches dropped off and rotting, the dividend
    of winter storms, the compounded interest of daylight.

High rises are the grief of the priests made tall and stable.
    Water flowing is proletariat, the people's portfolio.
    Abandon the World Trade Center. But where is the true
    center? Some bog where water stands warming, leveling
    a crook of hills with the valley beyond. Adam Smith,
    it is you who detached wealth from these watery glens.
    It is you who directed the evaporation of place.
    It is you, the first engineer of abstract markets.
    It is you I flow against with the pulse of spring flood.
    I sodden your *Wealth of Nations*. I mildew free markets,
    follow the meanders of the river of tribes, I spray
    the labor into one flow, flood the factories, erode
    the computer chips, wash out the self-interest of
    stockbrokers. I celebrate the falling Dow, and listen
    to the sound on a tin roof no one will insure. I watch
    as the water rises and the bridges are twisted into
    steel questions in the current. I bring the priest down
    from the temples. I found an order of initiates who
    watch the flow of rivers, calculate a science of eddies
    and waves. I call this market the Water Course Way.

THE BOTTOM LINE

"There's a crack in everything.
That's how the light gets in."
—LEONARD COHEN

There is a crack at the bottom, a simple equation for turning
    around and heading back toward the light. At the bottom
    the equation is factored into the dividends of speech
    and literacy. Plug in the numbers. Amortize
    the loan for the life I have chosen: poetry, passion.
    There is no bottom line to my speech of the heart.
    The prime rate is steady at seven. It's a good plan.

Sailing in the islands there is a door. It is where middle-aged
    men go through. It is the door past the bottom
    line. The wind is less a factor than the movement over
    waves. Women go inside to leave the bottom line behind.
    Men need movement over water, and the sadness
    of all the divorces. The mailman pushes letters into a spare
    room for years. The salesman pays off his second luxury
    car and feels empty in the drive-through. Bottom line?

The line is always forming at the rear. There is no balance
    sheet laid out sideways. There is a ship waiting
    at the dock called The Bottom Line. On board are three wise men
    from the east. Children learn their names at catechism.
    The boat is moored in a safe harbor. The sails folded
    on the deck. The wise men have berths of their own.
    They have taken off their suits and ties. They drink
    the local water, no checkbooks to balance. The ship
    is prepared to set sail over the decade to come.

DARKNESS

*"In Hindu theology, darkness is an aspect of
Kali as Time the destroyer."*
—THE ILLUSTRATED ENCYCLOPEDIA OF TRADITIONAL SYMBOLS

They will haul the instruments to the equator to measure
the speed of darkness. They wait for the final eclipse
of the sun to make the calculations. They march through
the rain forest toward the clearing in the trees where
delicate instruments will chart the progress of darkness
as it covers the sun. They believe in endarkenment.
They drive their cars to the airport on low beam.
They grow pale as cave salamanders. They calculate
to the nearest one thousand. They shift all the clocks
to daydark savings time, each day an hour shorter.

Darken the doorway. Darken the corner where you are. Take a
jump shot and really darken up the joint. Let there
be darkness in the tiniest theology. Let darkness stand
for all burned to ashes in the library at Alexandria.
In the dark a child wants none of the answers, but sits
spinning the calculations of maybe: maybe the first dark
is a time when the birds sing; maybe falling into
the mystery of black is the trick; maybe a mother approaches
the day from the wrong direction, from the hinges
of knowing what's on the grocery list, not the moon rising,
the moon with secondary light and primary darkness
on the backside; maybe dusk and dawn instead of reversed.

They arrive on the dark continent in air buses. They check
the boxes, fuel the trucks at the depot, depart
for the interior as night rises. Here the air is rich
in the nutrients of darkness: the sound of a foraging
bird, the smell of loam rotting in the shadows.
They drive through the night and sleep in guest houses
all day. They arrive at the clearing, set up delicate
machinery. I am with them in spirit. I court the chaos

of darkness. I align the bulbs and flip the switch,
plunging the classroom into darkness which passes
into settled peace in a moment. Don't replace the bulbs!
You there, from Westinghouse. Find employment
in the sector of darkness. Write a National Science Foundation
grant for moving all the universities to caves!
Walk the scientists deep into caverns with the blind.
Abandon flashlights at the entrance! Test the children
in the recognition of sounds in total darkness,
for that is an employable skill! Give up all sense
of knowing as light. Start at the beginning, the first dark
dollop. Write a new book. God has spoken again: Let there
be darkness. The primordial chaos ascending. The deluge
of unknowing. The delta of dark familiar speech.

In the forest the dawn is reversed into dusk. The celebration
of not seeing far. I am with them as they set up
the tripod where the pendulum swings. They wait
for the lightest hour, just before the dusk. They eat rations,
and drink from a nearby spring. Darkness is not
concentrated like the sun. It does not emanate from one
singular point, so they wait for it to appear
from the undersides of leaves where it waits out the day.
How to get a fix on it, creeping like spiders from every
leaf? The men are frantic in their deliberation. They
make their calculations in the shadows. Darkness has
no speed. It is not sudden nor is it the creeping shade.
The calculations pass from the notebooks to pencil
and back again. And it is dark again. Peaceful in the forest.

COLLEGE TEXTBOOKS

*"In twenty years you can recite everything
you can remember from college in five minutes."*
—FATHER GUIDO SARDUCCI

If you are in my class you may not purchase a textbook,
    you may not say text when you mean poems or stories,
    you may not sell your books back to the store upon
    completion of the syllabus. You must not complete
    the syllabus. Pile the uncompleted syllabi together
    in a back room and bind them at the spine. Call one
    pile the formula for the resolution of dreams, another
    incantations to bring back the dead. Sell these sacred
    books to freshmen, watch them worry over the black
    textured surface of required pages. Watch them pledge
    most of their life to pleasing, and file their marching
    orders with the pledge chairman. They consult the canon
    of behavior while dressing in the morning,
    they drink on the Row, they learn to stand in line
    and where to sit, they memorize who they can talk
    with, what they must read to pass. This is the moment
    of greatest disillusion. This is the moment when they
    have fallen closest to the nest. They are vulnerable
    to the predators, open to the singing sirens. They fumble
    in the dust with their large mouths open to whatever
    is offered from above. I do not feed them syllabi.
    They will never recover their body weight.

For sophomores, rearrange the pages and convince them
    you've gotten it exactly right. In the office laser the
    toner is low. Along the dark paths the carbon dusts the
    surface, like a late snow. The light is on. The
    machine's resident warning. Act now, but don't replace
    the cartridge, even if you find one on sale. Act as a rebel.
    Fill your head with inefficiency of whimsy, the static of
    bliss. Continue to print the syllabi until only a shadow
    remains, and finally the paper slides through the machine

completely white. Then hand these over, unbound to juniors.
Ask to hold them up to mirrors to read the secret code
of literature. Ask them to write in invisible ink. Give them
an address of a magic shop in the city and call that research.
Tell them this will be on the GRE, that their fraternity's
national chapter has an award for perfect erasure.
Tell them they win the game if they remember nothing
but the parties and the names of the officers.

It is time to assemble the senior slide show, the flashing
book of four years together, the shocking duration
of time. The seniors assemble all their syllabi, the coated
paper stiff from the chemical emulsion, the words
fading from freshman to senior year, the final blank
syllabus of the last semester. They work all night in
groups on the senior dinner's highest moment. The slides
are cued to Pearl Jam and Snoop Doggy Dogg. The movement
is syncopated. The pages of the syllabi move past:
Humanities, English 102, English 200, Art History,
Math 140, Science 101 & 102, French 201, P.E., History,
Philosophy, Religion. They throw in an old one, passed
down from a parent, brown on the edges, for nostalgia.

The seniors project the syllabi on the largest screen.
The chaplain sings the alma mater. The glee club closes
the awards ceremony with a rousing spiritual.
College is over. The syllabi for required courses dance
past in the dark. The seniors cry and imagine how much
they've learned. They transfer the slide show
to video tape. They pull the video syllabi out
of the drawer and view the tape at forty with a son
bound for college. They write the check. They grieve.

THE OLD PROFESSOR

And having fun? We'll have none of that.
Grades, grades, that's what they're here
for, the little slackers. There's even
talk of hiring a counselor. Nothing a few
hours in the library wouldn't cure
in their "psychology." Put the money
into books, proctors, testing material,
lock 'em in the dorms, board up fraternity
row, cut off all television reception
in the north quadrant of the city, then
you'll excite reliable cures in this college.

Service, by Jiminy. First to God, then family,
but third, before town, is gown. That's a value
we could use in class. College service, not fun.
You see this ring?
                    Haven't had it off in years.
It was given to me by my first college dean,
my fourth term, 1943. "Good service," is what's
engraved on the inside curve, close to the knuckle.
Good service. The college creed. Back then.

                    A handful of detractors
might say my life is like this ring, a small gold
circle grown too tight to slide. Especially
faculty meetings where I won't let anything
by, especially counselors and co-ed assistants.
Student affairs? Should be officed in the stacks.

And a football team? Nobody worth a damn
ever has one to brag about. I'd rather see
us whipped in Saturday combat, our eggheads
held high, than squander the college honor
on a winning season. You know what it means
to win today? It means, in **NCAA**, the boys
are thinking long and hard about **X** and **O**,

not Kierkegaard or "The Snows of Kilimanjaro."

Yes, I'm a gripe, an old one at that. It's time
to retire, bring the service to a close. But who
is left behind to guard the door? My colleagues?
As the old Quaker says, there's just thee and me,
and I've got my doubts about thee.
                                      Oh, the students?
They come and go, that's their nature, four years
in and then they're gone. It's constant
as the turning seasons, or the Hong Kong flu.
There've been good ones, but not in recent years.
Even the flow of a mighty river stops when the dam
of "activities" is placed so concretely across
the channel of intent, discipline, and will:
volleyball on a sand court, video rentals,
pizza parties every night. Is this summer camp,
MYF, or preparing the mind for serious study?

Pushing seventy, I sit in my stall, this old
office, and wait for the Dean to lay the shotgun
lightly in the hollow behind my ear. Retirement?
I won't give up without a fight. My world's been
sold down the river for a load of psychology,
happy children, and a winning football team.

THE WELL-ROUNDED STUDENT SPEAKS

Hell no I won't look
up the damn words I
don't know my head is
full enough thank you
and I don't need your
idea of knowledge
filling up spaces
easy things could
live comfortable
like brick houses in
the suburbs where all
six rooms have tvs
not those uppity
damn mansions with rooms
just for books.

If I knew just one more
fact beyond what I
know how much better
could I be? I had
an uncle who wished
he had one more ass-
hole than he has. They
called him crazy. So
if I wish for one
more thought then I'm just
as crazy as he
is. By the way did
you say this gonna
be on a test or
something? Then I'd best
remember—maybe—
especially if your test is hard.

SOONER THAN WE THINK

*sometime in the future,
in a place not far away*

The latest literary fauna survey shows only three breeding female semi-colons remain in the wild writing of undergraduates. An expedition under the auspices of the MLA attempted a penetration into the last remaining verdant prose in the lower 48, a small community college in Topeka, Kansas, but found little support for sightings of three male semi-colons cavorting in a research paper, trailing a pregnant female. In each case, the sighting was a comma splice; the trailing female, weighted heavily between two clauses, was believed to be some other mark of punctuation.

If the semi-colon's decline of habitat continues, it could mean extinction, the fate for certain of the once plentiful common apostrophe. Once, in early American prose there were so many apostrophes that it's said they darkened the page. An apostrophe, aging and bent, was spotted in a Harvard book review just before the turn of the century. Now nothing remains of the noble mark but a few stuffed lines in regional museums.

COUPLETS

I'd hire a miner to host the staffs of spring
if the winter didn't stagger home drunk on daffodils.

I'd cry foul if the wind demanded more than movement.
And if the grass headed the wrong way, I'd swear.

I'd like to know the umber of warmth with summer.
Stop the spring? Can't do. It comes on, no squeak.

Slip some down-and-out season a five and have it hail
me a cab. Call up summer on the cellular phone and cancel.

THE CAREER TRACK

I recommend the first groggy bee lifting from the purple
    violet. I honor the moment's attention, the creek
    current swirling in silted watery creases. This time
    of year, I stand dead still, walking the pollen path home.

I populate the neighborhoods with poplar leaves unfolding
    in resiny darkness. I cover the BMWs with early spring
    gravity's pollen sheen; I shake deep sleepers, pull
    them up to note the sun rising a minute earlier,
    setting a minute late. I shake marriages. Couples make
    love, then cry in the dark. I write tracts against day-
    light-saving time. I distribute them like a Jehovah's
    Witness. I take the pollen path from door-to-door.

This is the work to relocate the pollen path in what
    we call our growing older. I call the path our elder
    care plan. Invest monthly. Find the elders who know
    the steps. Activate them like soldiers hungry for a war.
    Get the troop ships out of mothballs and float them.
    Invest the platoons with the discipline of the soul's
    cadence. This path is not straight lines, or parade
    ground square. The pollen path wanders among the blooming
    hedgerows, not through them. The path is a slow
    invasion, like bees working from a hive. The elders lead
    the way like sergeants sure of their seasonal stripes.

In the grate, embers cool from the last winter fire.
    Spring fires are the pollen path, for curling up
    with a budding soul. I know the soul-time is not
    historical, but emotional. I walk the heart path too.
    I cry in cool spring shadows. I see the owl
    enter the tree like a knife and disappear. I wake
    in folds of darkness and hear the owl's first song.

SWEET TEA

God rested on the seventh day, but early in the morning,
    before the sun strained into the Southern sky,
    she made sweet tea from scratch. She boiled the water
    in a black kettle, put in the orange pekoe bags
    and let them stand as the water perked, and then
    she did what gods know to do: she heaped in Dixie
    Crystal sugar while the brew was still warm as the day.

For God so loved the world she made sweet tea. For she served
    the tea to anyone who admired her creation. To anyone
    walking down the street of the wet new neighborhood,
    to the mailman delivering early on that next day
    of that second week, to the milkman in his truck, the black
    man working in the yard, to the white man selling peaches
    door-to-door. On God's sidewalk there was an X scratched
    by hobos. They knew to come to God's back door and you'd
    get a plate of leftovers and all the sweet tea you could
    drink. They knew the sugared pints of contentment. They drank
    sweet tea from God's back steps and went on their wandering
    way again.

For God knows sweet tea fills with love and refreshment from
    any long train. For sweet tea is safe as an oak forest
    camp. Sweet tea, clinks in jelly jars. Sweet tea,
    sweeter as it stands. For God's sake we brew it
    like religion. For God's sake we carry it now in styrofoam
    cups in cars. We drink it in winter. We drink it always.

And this poem would not lessen sweet tea's place in the creation.
    Sweet tea is not fading from the Southern towns
    like the Confederate flag. It lives in houses all over town.
    Black folk brew it often as white folk. Take the flag off
    the state capitol. It doesn't mean anything to me.
    But leave be my sweet tea, a recipe for being civil.

This poem stands cold sweet tea up as God's chosen beverage.
> The manifest Southern brew. When sad I draw figures
> in the condensation of glasses of sweet tea. I connect
> the grape leaves on the jelly jar, cast out any restaurant
> that will not make it from scratch. When lonely I go
> to the house of my beloved.

For I love a woman who makes sweet tea late at night to eat with
> Chinese food. For her hands move like God's through the ritual.
> For it is as if she had learned it along with speaking in
> tongues. For I love the way her hands unwrap the tea bags
> and drop them in the water. For I love the unmeasured sugar
> straight from the bag, the tap water from deep in the earth.
> For these processes are as basic for love as making love.
> For our bodies both are brown like suntans inside from years
> of tea. For sweet tea is the Southern land we share, the town,
> the past. When we kiss it is sweet tea that we taste as
> our lips brush. When we are hot it is sweet tea we crave.
> When we have children it will be sweet tea.
> And they will learn tea along with Bible stories and baseball.

DEATH

*"Death may come in many forms, they say, but truly
it comes in only one, which is the end of love."*
        —HAYDEN CARRUTH

Warm for a week, the new moon two weeks away,
        another spring storm moving in from the west,
sparrows choosing aimlessly among debris in the yard,
        as if winter had suddenly vanished. I imagine
he—the man I'm always writing about—is watching
        sparrows on a similar evening, far from home,
the sales job where he is often promoted. But it's
        the parking lot of a Wendy's on the outskirts
of Charlotte. He is my age, but older really, the way
        men age who take life seriously, stock portfolios,
suits, and cars with high resale value, a wife, children.

He has ordered off the Value Menu, a Single, large fries,
        an ice tea. Outside, sparrows dismantle a corner of bun
among the gravel and he thinks of a young woman
        in his regional office, just out of college, and how
when he sees her, each week, he remembers making love
        to his wife the first time, the desire sunk so deep
even a sparrow could not peck it out. He flirts
        a little, and once, in an elevator they were pushed
so close that he thought desire would explode from within,
        her grey suit and pantyhose blown away with one glance.

Spring is a tiny death, I say, with much joy. The slumber
        of winter falling away as chills drain back into
the earth from which they came. There are sprouts
        in the yard conjuring summer, slumbering worms.
This man within me, he has three more stops to make
        before circling home for the evening. He thinks
of the young woman in the office a final time, a last
        French fry from his Value Meal. Does she eat
alone? With friends from the office? His wife waits,
        the furnace set at 65, dinner on the stove.
I get up to make coffee a final time this morning,
        another set of grounds for the compost. I would
never choose to be anywhere but here.

II. EVEN IN DOGGEREL THERE IS THIS SEED

> "Roaring dreams take place in a perfectly silent
> mind. Now that we know this, throw the raft away."
> —JACK KEROUAC

THE EARLY DECADES

There is an infinite sadness to any truth,
like the brittle slide of metal when the temperature
drops to forty below. This is the decade
men warm hands in pockets, passing
whiskey back and forth through a window
open to the weather, to what they might feel.

The men walk away, cannot entirely feel
semblances of that viable structure of truth,
the average furniture in a culture's window
always blocks away. They gauge the temperature
from inside a room, after a long day passing
in the streets and alleyways of a public decade.

A century has passed since men sat for a decade
at their high desks, like Bartleby, and feel
the essential creases of their livelihood passing
like carriages in the street: cluttered, a truth,
seasonal and an intramural pleasure, like the temperature.
But even from where he sat, a man could close the window.

He stood at the curtains, the blunted noise, the window
open to the traffic and his generation, a decade
sluicing in his veins, his human temperature
all that warmed his hands, digits that feel
so far from the stove, the cast iron like glowing truth.
A century of faith stopped in the streets, passing.

All is worn away in the narrative's time, passing
like men and carriages in the open window.
Now men trust other documents of truth,
labels on bottles, computer screens, the garbage of decades.
All interested in print or history can feel
the moody bus, legal certainties, the temperature.

The men have left the room, the years, the temperature
adjusted like the stock market; all the intuition passing
into systems of delusion, made possible by a century's feel
for dismissed registrars in the floorboard, the open window.
Men can stand their lonely offices for a decade
or two but will always shuffle toward some truth.

Oh, for a truth, some reading of the temperature.
Higher than the early decades. Just watch the men passing,
and account for the feel of heaving bodies in the window.

HAMMERED LEAVES

*After seeing a 17th Century Japanese arrowhead
with intricate landscapes carved within at the
Metropolitan Museum*

The old man carving at his bench, the bamboo's intricate
joinery, a hillside, delicate hammered sheaf of leaves,
and the blade's perfect edge. And then the craftsman
lays down his tools on the table, the day's war over,
this weapon completed, the smoke of craft clearing finally
in the breezy workshop behind the prince's winter palace.

He knows war and art are initial disciplines a palace
sponsors, the landscape altered, all truth intricate
within the prince's walls. The old craftsman's art is finally
mastered, years at the carving, but the steel leaves
him dead to the touch of women, a soldier crossed over
the river, into the mist of battle, one of culture's craftsmen.

So he walks into the street, buys a dumpling, now craftsman
to his belly's ache, carving long, acid's groaning palace
his only thought. The dumpling is moist in his hand. Over
in Hokkaido, where he learned his fury, his lasting intricate
way with bamboo and delicate peaceful landscapes, his leaves
with so little thin metal the wind moves them. He eats finally,

and his stomach stops its ache, his mind quiets, finally.
He is a warrior for the prince, an old man, a craftsman,
the first of the Hokkaido guild to master hammered leaves,
so he left the provinces, settled his workshop in the palace.
Even the dumpling reminds him of hammering, the intricate
dimpled edging. Art of war on dough. War is never over.

The street darkens, and merchants hawk their wares over
tables built from the prince's untaxed mountain oak. Finally
even commerce is at war with the prince, the intricate
mind working, an arrow in a wound. The prince, a craftsman,

his soldiers hammered steel, and all who squat in the palace
so many warriors of the prefect's royal whim, so many leaves.

When the craftsman turns down his street, his feet and leaves
are distant below him. A veteran returned from over
there, war in service of the prince, his cluttered palace
workshop of arrowheads finished and half-finished, finally
all that lasts is private, perfect carving of the craftsman.

War is an intricate state of being, but the hammered leaves
of the craftsman are a private combat, carved over and over
by the old artist. He dies, but not in service of the palace.

SIX WORDS OFF A POSTCARD BY NIN ANDREWS

In the reproduction of wild seals what
matters is the success of the program.
It's cold in the far north, and intimate
relations on frozen marsh grass
tend to speed things up, or write
off petting as an option. Humans want more.

This morning there were many more
grackles in the garden. Exactly what
I would call a flock. As I write
this poem, caught in a repeating program
of words, I think of the far north grass,
holding the shape of seals. How intimate.

Below the surface, soil is warm, intimate
I'd say. Even as a worm I'd expect more
than one brief crawl through sprouting grass.
Two long bodies, love's repeated approach, what
we humans call desire. Get with the program.
Expect to surface in the rain while you write.

For poets it always comes to this, to write
on winter mornings alone among these intimate
verbs such as sprout. I set up the program
and let it play through, always return for more,
repeating the seal, lumbering overland toward what
mystery of biological preparation is in the cold grass.

Too much. This stanza I will avoid the love grass,
the grackles and the worm. I will only write
of the sestina's mystery of repetition. And what
profit this, losing the freedom of the intimate?
Of the stanzas this one is the one more
abstract you would say. Not part of the program.

Grass warmed, bent double in love, is the program.
Do not mistake the poem, or the word grass
or speaking of it for love. I, simply human, want more.
If not making love, seal or worm, I write.
Language pushed to the heat of poetry is intimate,
but bodies drawn together, worm or seal, is what

I consider of greater importance, what the program
calls *now,* I call *intimate.* Fall to the grass.
Make love more. And then, goddamn it, write.

THE MAP

"The territory no longer precedes the map."
—JEAN BAUDRILLARD

1.
Though years since I visited the area of the map,
the territory lies folded in my pocket for reference.
Bearings are difficult, the lines denoting elevation,
how to read them again? The endless geodetic coordinates,
the perfect grid laid over the green and white skin
of the map. But then I remember: the central intersection
of squares, a place I know: flat, measured, no surprises.

2.
The territory is not needed, so I leave it folded.
I move along the contours of the map with ease.
A left here, and there, a right. But sometimes
the territory's memory emerges, almost a place,
some rough crease like a draw where the map was folded
years before, persistent in a way print never can be.
I pause, remembering again. The smell of a flower,
the way dirt gathers. Wind on an imminent crop of wheat.

3.
Disoriented by my senses, I stand in relation to the map.
I stand for minutes, or hours, for time no longer precedes
the clock. I stand waiting for a thought, but thought
no longer precedes the thinker. I stand. I listen.

4.
I admit I am lost, take out the territory, unfold it
carefully between squares 5779 and 6240. It is burly
and unmanageable, the way loam feels in your hands.
What is the name of this promontory to my left?
The name of this precipitous draw? The territory is mute
in a way the map never is, unfolds, filling one corner
of the sector. Is that the horizon? I say. I slowly fold
the map, walk toward the language by which I've lived.

CONNEMARA

after a Steichen photograph of the Sandburgs

Maybe they sit outside, after feeding the goats.
She still adores him, the poet, the man with guitar
player's fingers and white hair of the far north.
His blue eyes focus off somewhere to the left,
and he holds the guitar as if a minor chord
he used to know, the difficult one, has escaped.

He has been playing folk songs. The words escaped
somehow from the mountains around them, like goats
loose in the hickory woods. And the last chord
to linger in the air drifts back toward the guitar
and settles like dust from a mote just to the left
of where her hand would rest were it extended north.

They lived for fifty years near Chicago, way north
of Connemara, but then they packed papers, escaped
the cold and the memory of the old work with the Left.
Now less interested in politics, more in baby goats,
he strums at old labor tunes on a battered guitar.
If only he could remember the tone of that lost chord.

When he was a boy he only learned one simple chord
a day, and stopped after a week. In the north,
where he grew up, in a railroad town, an old guitar
was less useful than a signal lantern. If you escaped
you did it by train. That slight shadow, is it goats?
Something dark does wander in the photo to the left.

By the photo's moment, he's finished Lincoln, the Left
abandoned, home and poetry, his song book's true chord.
She works in the barn. The first prizes won by goats
garland the rafters in her office. Up there, north,
it is only the cold she thinks they had escaped
when they drove the truck south with stock and guitar.

For the photograph, he picks up the old guitar
and she takes her place just to the photo's left.
The goats, except for a shadow, have almost escaped
and silence is the shudder caught between the chord
lost and the chord abandoned. It's cold in the north
and she always claimed the south is better for goats.

A man once played guitar. His life was one chord.
What's lost in the photo. Later he forgot the north,
escaped the frame, the fence, like a mountain goat.

NOSTALGIA FOR WORK AND DEEP MOUNTAINS

Along the broad valleys peasants extend a history
of potatoes and wheat. Each steady worker, evening
folding behind him, pushes barrows like boats
over rutted trails to home, smoke spiraling, like messages
rising off the river of dawn, the blue haze
in the distance, the woods on the mountainside.

A short man slowly scratches his curving side,
as if the spot held affection for him, a history
of skin and hand, white ridge meeting slab of blue
nail; this is the final hour before another evening
unfolds its comfort and soup speaks its quiet message,
the bowls waiting on the table, spoons deep as frigates.

He climbed the rigging once, not long schooners
but tall ships, and his size kept him to the side
of the mast, where the ropes bowed and the messages
were hung with signal flags. He remembers no history
as he walks into the yard on this normal evening,
no special day to mourn often as the hills turn blue.

He notices his wife has set the evening table, blue
bottoms of the soup bowls, the deep curve of dories
bobbing on a calm sea shocks him free of evening,
and the frightening fall, plunging over the side
into the sea; he is a farmer now with no history
to sidle into—soup only—domestic messages.

His wife sends her clear love through the messages
of soup and table; if the spoon is clean, it is blue,
and this event she chronicles in the long history
of this valley; she knows not his memories of sloops,
or even the tiny scar scripting his burly right side
though her hands stay steady on his back late evening.

The short man conjures his way back to escaping evening,
sends out a flutter of soft homely literal messages,
his blue, rheumy eyes cast on the hearth to the side,
where the fire burns like red rigging in the rough blue
granite of the firebox, the stones cut into harsh vessels
of heat by the practice of it all, the domestic history.

This is a man and woman's history. Every evening
they moor together like launches, reading signal messages:
blue for storm, white for fair, listing side-to-side.

GOOD FENCES

My neighbor, mad, stood on his stoop and yelled,
Fuck it. Was it yapping chow puppies in his backyard,
or some awful news come down in mail or rumor?
He's told me all he wants: a little quiet, a shift man,
with beer to drink and games to watch. The puppies
duck for cover, then whine and gamble through the uncut

shrubs and scrap wood along our mutual line of fence.
He stomps back inside. Loud barks drift in
to move me, little lions in the shrubs. Now he's
gone, the yard is safe for noise again. Once he
slammed a skillet on the head of a cruising horny cur,
the father of this litter. It was Super Bowl Sunday,

and I could hear them there, screaming for Dallas.
So he let the chow out to piss, and the cur mounted her.
They walked the back yard, tail to tail, howling
an hour before he forgot the game, realized she was out.
He crushed the dog's skull, pulled them apart, and threw
the carcass in the street to rot. January kept it from

smelling until the city picked it up, dumped it only God
knows where. Good fences make good neighbors,
and I've thought of putting up a wood one six feet high,
painting Frost there. You know, get some art students,
some beer, take a Sunday, and make the mural cover
the whole damn thing, not caring what meanness goes on

behind it ever again. I know he'd never see it,
never know I'm looking at some poet on the other side.
But I've got to see the puppies through, and the wire
fence is the trick, though watching them is hard:
they fight like hell. He comes out to yell every night.
It seems I've accepted I'll never know what wire
is scratching at his insides anymore than he'll know mine.
So we get along. I throw scrap wood over the fence
for him to burn in his wood stove. When the wind shifts,
smoke from his chimney drifts in here. Fence or not,
we're close. So Frost was right: good fences do make
good neighbors, though they come in every shape and size.

CHILDHOOD & LINGUISTICS

"In France children know that words and meaning are not connected, that train is a short word for a long object, and cigarette is a long word for a short object..."
—NEW YORK TIMES

I suspected early on I had a career in linguistics. Was God too small a word for an infinite being? I asked this question walking to school. I believe I was eight at the time. And then, with a little twist of my elementary logic, I saw that spelled backward, the word is even small for the barking presence left behind in my back yard.

And where to go next? Pushed forward by the babble of children at recess, I would take the word god apart, spread its three pieces across the dirt, pronouncing in my loneliness the dangling sweep of g, a small sound for a large rush of air, the o, infinitely hollow as I fell through the hole, and the stiff d, standing on its own like the school's flagpole weighted down with a bag of sand.

I gave up on my career in linguistics in sixth grade, when I chanted *the* over and over on my back in the attic until word and meaning separated like the cuffs on my best dress pants. *The, the, the, the, the, the*...So how could God stand a chance against a childhood of linguistics? Simple articles torn apart in the spin of my childlike centrifuge.

MY DEAD FATHER SURVEYS THE PATTERNS

He never was much for sewing, but my dead father
is back for an instant at the yard sale. He rummages
through a box of old patterns stacked like corpses.
He tosses them over his skinny shoulder into the yard.
What is he after? What's so important down there
at the bottom of the box? Some old lady stored
these patterns in the late Fifties, placed the box
on a shelf and left it. She never pulled it down
until today when we all showed up, my dead father
briefly among us, looking for a bargain like the living.

Now he's found it, a brown paper padding the bottom.
He's reading the old news in the yard like he's bored.
November 15th, 1959, my father reads. It's the day
he's killed himself, back then. He shows me the article.
It's the pattern he wants to take back with him. It's all
he came back for. He offers the lady a quarter for the paper,
but she doesn't hear. Thank God he's quick to be on his way.

SOMEDAY MY MOTHER'S DEATH

will be the mistletoe in the oak, will be the way mistletoe
sends out runners in the living wood, the way it stays green
when everything around it is brown, will be her stories popping
white berries in our memories, especially Christmas, how even
after the mistletoe kills the oak it goes on living high
in the tree for years.
                      And the old woman when she dies
will remember the persistence of mistletoe, the rough leaves
of the mistletoe which settle on the walk in the wind,
sprigs of mistletoe good for nothing beyond the everyday
pleasure of looking out the upstairs window into the highest
branches, choked with mistletoe, sad with mistletoe, last
great breath of oak before the mistletoe goes the way of oak.

THE MUSE IS LOOKING FOR

One poet, male, female or other, with language
skills in: clumsy palpable recall, rough play,
persistence, greased repetition, the shins of desire,
passions, chance, idiot affections, the rolling ardor
of rejection, the eminent domain of sex and death,
roaming the happy, happy Africas of their mammal heart.

Early riser preferred who is willing to work
mornings or evenings (i.e. see the sun's comings and goings)
on poems no matter the weather, date, day or other
professional, community or (wife, husband, children ok)
family responsibilities. Must listen and ignore.

No experience necessary, but upon application
must be willing to begin immediately traveling, walk,
or saunter, traverse, trek, trip, and tread, or stay deadly
boring put, depending on the need, depending on the day.

RHETORIC

Someone should have told me
my chosen verbs could not collapse
into a spinning green memory,

and that I could follow my nouns
back to their source, the yellow
root cooling beneath the oak.

My adverbs hunker dark & deep
in the loam. The participle
phrase, like a snail, glistens

over a board slick with melted
frost. That crystal leveler
of the moist life will return

tomorrow night, and the snail's
shiny carapace slowly undulates
with the new urgency of cold

rising from the syntax of earth.
Leech from me not my vegetable prose;
it kicks like larvae in the shaded tank.

In my grammar's yard the expected sun
is rising. The first rays arriving
like pairs of geese from the far north.

What flies can also land, slow birth,
new decay; and language cavorts
in this morning's rising voice of heat.

DOGGEREL

The news this morning from Mexico

The language of tropical wood & Mayan craftsmanship conspires somewhere in Chiapas to clean the barrel of an AK-47, to cultivate the *milpa* of revolution. This morning, Mexico's hills are loud as irregular verbs, and the people, poor as slash and burn.

It is not a language they seek, but poetry could break out in the rain forest of their voices at any moment to export the shiny seeds of their indigenous grievance. Even in doggerel there is this seed, like the cure for cancer waiting in the forest, the last crocodile surfacing in a small pond off the Ucumacinta.

Do you understand what they ask? Not doggerel but food. Fair prices for corn. And it has come to this again. Always the assumption of power. Always the army who speaks in doggerel too. The whole conversation not like a cafe, but like a street vendor, waiting to sell a hammock. The price headed down, down.

THEORY IN A PUBLIC PLACE

Curry wafts from the kitchen. The air smells yellow. *But even food had to begin as theory*, he speculates, pleased with himself, breaking open a steaming crescent of *nan*. From here it is not far to the kitchens of Postmodernism. Language cooked, served up, smothered in the sauces of theory. The death warrant signed, sentence passed on literature, he stews the others in a spicy loud deconstruction, serves up the rice of grievance.

The plates of real *sag* congeal as he butts heads with the editor, the poet, and then a man at the next table stands, says: *all I know is that what's wrong with this country is people like you all with your big words and black clothes and I paid good money to come here and eat with my wife and when we order chicken curry we get chicken curry and so there must be something being said and the waiter's a goddamn Indian for Christ sake so screw you with all that shit about words not meaning you listening mister because I ain't saying it again I for one don't sit around and think about Derrida who the hell ever she is but instead how I'll pay my bills this month and this meal will cost me over twenty dollars so shut the fuck up while we eat.*

LOGGING

FOR JIM PETERSON

In spring loam offers
a grove constant humming
like the bee's glade
humus parts and sleeves
of seedlings inch along
we dream them seeds
saplings yearlings
dream them grown thick
as this oak or that
thorn on the wild rose

If lucky we dream a walk out
a door wandering hours toward
that humming spring grove
not turning past turnip fields
controlled burns pruned
peaches but on toward stands
of hardwood and a burly river
cutting down deep muddy nearby
follow that spring river over
roots and carbuncles
of last year's rotted leaves
wade hours shallow crossings
noisy shoals collapsed
cut bank from grove to grove

This is as close as I want
to be to silence impulsive
vegetable needs waiting
us out to wander past
not the saw's frenzy our
words progressing toward
the blank milled pages
but the factories of sawdust
stumps slash second growth

Poetry is always new loam
we the logger one and another
the sacred groves broken under
the red skidder's ribbed tires

SAILBOAT

Come
closer, he said
in his bold Magellan way.
Her toes the nearest thing like
a continent's cape imagined from a distance.
Feet like charts never lie. Especially, two feet,
like sails in the wind. Five toes on each foot, like a
crew waving from the dock. The first sock off, then the next.
It's
down to two bare feet, sailors too long at sea. She blushes.
*I have a ring on my toe. Crossing the International Date
Line in a sailboat.* A small silver ring in the lamp
light. He pulls her foot forward to suck her
bold mysterious toes.

ABOUT THE AUTHOR

John Lane was born October 29th, 1954, the son of Mary Brown Lane, waitress, and John Edwards Lane, service station owner, in Southern Pines, North Carolina. Almost all schooling in Spartanburg, South Carolina, his mother's ancestral home. College at Wofford, English and Religion major, then ten years on the road: Breadloaf, Belize, Port Townsend, Copper Canyon Press, pizza and beer in a dark pool bar on Water Street. Then Virginia: UVA, Hoyns Fellow, cooking in Charlottesville, and on to cook in wilderness, Cumberland Island. Finally back to South Carolina and North Carolina piedmont and mountains, kayaking, writing. Back to Spartanburg, teaching at Wofford College: literature, creative writing, and film. Now home again, settled in, he is publisher/editor of Holocene Press.